THE LORD DELIGHTS IN YOU

Caitlyn Ray Edamer

TABLE OF CONTENTS

TABLE OF CONTENTS

INTRODUCTION

This book was written to encourage anyone living in darkness, feeling stuck, or completely overwhelmed. I have been there. I have been there, wondering what my purpose was or if I was taking the proper steps. I have been there in depression and filled with anxiety. I have been overwhelmed by the pressures of society and the pressures I may have put on myself.

I write all this to say: You are not alone.

In all that you may face, you are not alone. I write this to bring you hope and to inform you of the living hope that is Jesus!

In my life, I have struggled so much with freedom, peace, life, and purpose. I was previously bound to darkness and living in swirling chaos. I have broken free of living in darkness, and because I know other people are stuck in their darkness, I want to share the stories that have helped me. My life was transformed when I began to live in joy and love fully!

This book is filled with encouraging written words similar to essays or blog entries, supported by Bible stories. I will refer to the Christian Standard Bible throughout the Biblical text we will cover in this book. Referring to the Word of God will not only help you in challenging circumstances, but these stories will continue to remind you how wonderful and faithful our God is in all life's circumstances. These stories will light your path to freedom. I pray that through this book, you are set entirely free. I pray that each reader who picks up this book would encounter the living God, know how loved they are, and know there is hope in this life. I pray that each person experiences peace that surpasses all understanding and fullness of joy that can only come from knowing God.

1

Jesus loves YOU

Jesus was a perfect and sinless man, born of a virgin. His life and death changed the world. He lived a life full of service, kindness, and love. His death rattled the Earth, and darkness poured in. He died and went down to Hell and conquered death! He rose again to life and then ministered to his disciples and others for forty days until he ascended into Heaven. He gave us the gift of the Holy Spirit so He would always be with us.

He did not die, conquer death, and come back to life for no reason.. It's because He loves us. What a gift of love He gave us! Jesus said to love one another and that to love someone is to lay their life down for another. He did that for us! He experienced all the emotions we may experience as humans and can relate to and understand us well. He was God in human form.

In John 3:16-17, it is written, "For God loved the world in this way: He gave his one and only Son, so that everyone who believes in him will not perish but have eternal life. For God did not send his Son into the world to condemn the world, but to save the world through him."

Jesus paid the penalty of sin for us because our debt was so much greater.

"Death has been swallowed up in victory. Where, death, is your victory?
Where, death, is your sting?
The sting of death is sin, and the power of sin is the law. But thanks be to God, who gives us the victory through our Lord Jesus Christ!"
1 Corinthians 15:55-57

We have victory in Jesus' name! How exciting is that?

When one fully understands how loved they are, it changes them. I pray that each reader would encounter the Holy Spirit and experience the fullness of God's love.

God created us uniquely different and wonderful, and He loves who we are at this moment. How precious are His thoughts about us! He created you with intention and purpose! You were made for a time such as this!

"For it was you who created my inward parts; you knit me together in my mother's wom. I will praise you because I have been remarkably and wondrously made. Your works are wondrous and I know this very well."
Psalm 139:13

So not only did the Creator of the Heavens and Earth think that the world needed you, but He also sent His son to die for you! You have the honor of walking in full freedom because of God's amazing love for you!

2

Broken Shackles

Romans 6:6-11 says, "For we know that our old self was crucified with him so that the body ruled by sin might be rendered powerless so that we may no longer be enslaved to sin, since a person who has died is freed from sin. Now if we died with Christ, we believe that we will also live with him, because we know that Christ, having been raised from the dead, will not die again. Death no longer rules over him. For the death he died, he died to sin once for all time; but the life he lives, he lives to God. So, you too consider yourselves dead to sin and alive to God in Christ Jesus."

Take a moment to take in the power of that passage. YOU are free from sin. Death has no hold on you or your life! You are alive in Christ! There may be times when you struggle with sin, but it has no dominion over you! And you have the gift of the Holy Spirit to overcome any temptation or struggle.

When we are enslaved to sin, we are bound and held down wearing shackles. The shackles of sin are heavy, but Jesus is the key to unlocking them, and we can walk freely. We are not struggling for victory, we have that! Remember 1 Corinthians 15? Death has been swallowed up in victory!

I have this picture in my mind of a child carrying all their school books in their backpack: History, Science, Social Studies, and English. They are heavy! They pull on the backpack's straps and hurt their back while carrying everything. The part of this picture that gets me is when the sweet child turns to their guardian and asks for help with the load they are carrying.

Matthew 11:30 says, "For my yoke is easy and my burden is light." The burden becomes light when we turn to Jesus and ask for help with whatever we carry. We can stand tall. Whether it is sin, pressure from society, or a heavy workload, Jesus has our backs- literally. He is our friend who will walk alongside us and help us!

3

God's Protection

Our haven is in the arms of God. He is the "Good Shepherd" of our souls. We are safest when we turn to Him. Psalm 23:4 says, "Even when I go through the darkest valley, I fear no danger, for you are with me; your rod and your staff - they comfort me."

When I read that verse, I am reminded that God brings the ultimate comfort. I may seek comfort from things of this world or in other people, but when I seek God for comfort, He brings an indescribable peace. I can seek refuge in His Spirit when I am grieving, worried, or depressed. No matter the emotion I feel, He is there. His heart is full of compassion and care for his children.

There was a time in my life when I would have nightmares, and the darkness from depression would feel so heavy in my chest. But I know for a fact that God was near and protecting me. He surrounded me when I felt alone.

Reflecting on that time, I feel joy now to know that I no longer have to live in fear because He is with me!

No matter the circumstances you may face, God is surrounding you with His Spirit. He is at work to keep you safe. He is the all-knowing and all-powerful living God; He has your back.

Joshua 1:9 says, "Haven't I commanded you: be strong and courageous? Do not be afraid or discouraged, for the Lord your God is with you wherever you go." That is a command! You no longer need to live in fear; God leads you! He is our strength when we are weak. You are in the safety net of His arms. He cares about you. Even the tiny, minuscule things, He cares!

If you were to close your eyes, hold your hands together, and lean back without reaching, would you trust someone to catch you? Do you know who would catch you every single time? The Lord!

What does trust look like to you? In trusting Him, we know we are safe from all things. He will cover us and protect us. In each step of our lives, He is there.

He will never leave your side. So, practice the trust fall. You can fall safely into His arms.

4

Get Out of That Grave

In Matthew 28, an angel shares with the women who were going to view Jesus' tomb, "Don't be afraid, because I know you are looking for Jesus who was crucified. He is not here. For he has risen". He is risen! What fantastic news for the women and us today!

It is time to wake up! Wake up to the good news that He is risen! Not only has He risen, but because of the blood shed on the cross, we are free! It is time to get up out of that grave you have been living in and rejoice in His goodness!

I pray that the graves of despair, sorrow, or sadness would be no more! We are called to a life of joy and abundance! Hell and darkness have no place here.

"But God, who is rich in mercy, because of his great love that he had for us, made us alive with

Christ even though we were dead in trespasses. You are saved by grace!"
Ephesians 2:4-5

His grace fully and completely saves us. The gracious and forgiving love given to us is greater than any gift anyone could ever give us. Our merciful God blessed our lives by sending us His son. We no longer have to sulk in depression. We are called to rejoice that "He is risen!"

How do we reflect this in our daily lives? When I imagine myself walking out of that grave of despair, I see praise being brought to the Lord. A gleeful and joyful shout! It is good that we no longer have to live there. That grave does not belong to us anymore! Imagine walking through life with full hope for the future, knowing you are loved beyond measure!

5

Manna

"It was white like coriander seed and tasted like wafers made with honey," describes manna in Exodus 16:31. For forty years, the Israelites ate manna. They were tired, hungry, and wanted more. God provided the exact amount of manna they needed to survive and thrive. They ate this in the wilderness before they reached the land of plenty.

When we are hungry and need more, God will provide. If we try to do it ourselves and it isn't from God, it can become spoiled. It will not mean the same. When the Israelites tried to save more manna for the next day, it began to stink and was full of maggots. God will provide exactly what you need for the season you are currently in. Nothing more and nothing else. Exactly what you need.

I bring this story of the manna up because imagine the peace you can have in your life when you trust that God will provide everything. We need to not worry about what worries the next day will bring, for the Lord will provide, protect, and lead us.

The Lord will find unique ways to provide, whether through a person, a new opportunity, or a miraculous way. He will find a way, and He will do it!

6

Surpasses All Things

"Don't worry about anything, but in everything, through prayer and petition with thanksgiving, present your requests to God. And the peace of God, which surpasses all understanding, will guard your hearts and minds in Christ Jesus. Finally, brothers and sisters, whatever is true, whatever is honorable, whatever is just, whatever is pure, whatever is lovely, whatever is commendable—if there is any moral excellence and if there is anything praiseworthy—dwell on these things. Do what you have learned and received and heard from me, and seen in me, and the God of peace will be with you. Philippians 4:6-9

   This passage reveals that the thoughts we have and things we may worry about, we can take to God! With a thankful heart, we can present our worries to Him. The tricky part for some is not dwelling on what we worry about. Instead of dwelling on your daily trials and tribulations, focus on the goodness in the trials. Having a grateful heart may sometimes feel challenging, but concentrating on the beautiful things in life that God has blessed us with makes it easier to get through those challenging moments.

This passage describes the peace of God to surpass all things and all understanding. I did not live in peace for a long time, but a huge weight was lifted when I fully surrendered my worries to God. This can be the same for you, too. It did not make sense that I was no longer worried about finances or my job's stability. I trusted the all-knowing God and knew He would make a way. There is no one like Him!

He is our Father in heaven. He knows and loves you so much and wants you to live a life full of grace and love. He created you! Why would He have done so if He did not intend to care for you all your life? He will always lead and guide you in a way that will bring you peace. Trust in His unfailing word and love. He provided for the Israelites for forty years; He will also provide for you.

7

The Wildflowers

Matthew 6 is full of some good reading. In verses 25-34, it is generally speaking of anxiety. The command of the passage is this: "Don't worry about your life, what you will eat or what you will drink; or about your body, what you will wear. Isn't life more than food and the body more than clothing?" A few examples in the passage demonstrate how faithful God is and that we do not need to worry..

Those examples included in this passage are of the birds of the sky and the wildflowers of the field. They do not worry where their next meal comes from, what they will look like tomorrow, or what the future holds. They all trust in God to provide.

The beauty of these examples is this: you are worth more than the birds of the sky and the wildflowers of the field. Your life, desires, and cares are essential to God; He will provide every need. We no longer have to stress!

The passage concludes, "Therefore, don't worry about tomorrow, because tomorrow will worry about itself. Each day has enough trouble of its own." Only God knows what the future holds. He knows how to care for and prepare us for the next moment. Seeking God and turning to Him before our worries will result in us living where trust, humility, and love are displayed!

There is a song I listen to titled "Birds" by Anna Golden. It goes like this: "Birds in the air, they don't worry. The sun's never scared that it won't rise. If all of creation depends on your goodness, why, oh why can't I? Anxiety is such a human thing, but what do the creatures know about you?" I listen to this song when I need a reminder of Matthew 6. Anna is so right. What is it about creation that they can fully trust in God's goodness? If all of God's creatures trust Him, why is it so hard for us to do that? Lord, teach us to be like the birds in the air, to trust you like they do!

8

Be Still

When you feel toppled with stressor after stressor, turn to Mark 4:35-41. The passage says, "On that day, when evening had come, he told them, 'Let's cross over to the other side of the sea.' So they left the crowd and took him along since he was in the boat. And other boats were with him. A great windstorm arose, and the waves broke over the boat, so the boat was already swamped. He was in the stern, sleeping on the cushion. So they woke him up and said to him, 'Teacher! Don't you care that we're going to die?' He got up, rebuked the wind, and said to the sea, 'Silence! Be still!' The wind ceased, and there was a great calm. Then he said to them, 'Why are you afraid? Do you still have no faith?' And they were terrified and asked one another, 'Who then is this? Even the wind and the sea obey him!'"

There is only one who brings complete peace to our hearts. Jesus is the one whom the wind and sea obey! In this passage, the disciples were worried about the raging storm and that their boat might tip over. Life can feel like this, too, almost like you are drowning with responsibilities and pressure from society or yourself.

Jesus questions the disciples, "Why are you afraid?" Why are you afraid today? Are you scared of being toppled? Do you fear you are not good enough? Let me tell you this, you are good enough! You are never given more than you can handle. Jesus loves who you are and what you are doing. He is our friend we can turn to and be real with, no matter what we are feeling or experiencing.

Imagine this: The Son of God, whom the wind and seas listen to, will always be with you! All you need to do is be still and trust. He is with you, He is near, and He is for you! When life may feel impossible, you can hand him whatever you are struggling with. He is our Helper!

9

Hope

. . . .

Days can feel like they are dragging on. The mundane school tasks, long working hours, or a chaotic household may feel tiring. It can feel like rest may never come, but do not worry, because the ultimate rest and peace is found in Psalm 62:5-6, "Rest is in God alone, my soul, for my hope comes from Him. He alone is my rock and salvation, my stronghold; I will not be shaken." Time spent with God is healing for the heart and will allow us to have hope for whatever tomorrow may bring.

When I reflect on Psalm 62:5-6, I am reminded of a passage in Matthew 7, which discusses building your house on the rock. It says to be wise and strong, for the foundation you place your life on will impact you. If God is your rock and you stand firm in His plan, you will have hope. His goodness and faithfulness are displayed in the plans for your life; all you need to do is trust His plans!

To not be shaken means to stand firm in faith. You must stand tall! You know that you can get through anything with the God of hope on your side.

A life without hope is a life without trusting in God and believing His plans for you are good. My prayer for you is stated in Romans 15:13, "May the God of hope fill you with all joy and peace in believing, so that by the power of the Holy Spirit you may abound in hope."

I can testify that He was with me and showed me that there was joy and fullness in His plans when the walls crumbled around me, and I did not have hope. I am thankful for His unwavering love. Our God will never fail us; He is for us!

10

Light in the Darkness

Jesus is the true light of the world. Because of Him, we are called to be a light. The world can feel dark and scary but can be overcome with hope, peace, and love. Matthew 5:15 says, "No one lights a lamp and puts it under a basket, but rather on a lampstand, and it gives light for all who are in the house."

God created us to be the light for others struggling in darkness. To love people who may be struggling and give yourself some grace. Please do not be ashamed of the bright light you are; embrace it! Your light is so bright, it cannot be hidden! The light that lives in you will change the world!

When I imagine what light looks like, I imagine radiating joy, peace, and hope. Jesus gives us hope to move forward and is a living example of what that light looks like. In John 8:12, Jesus says, "I am the light of the world. Anyone who follows me will never walk in the darkness but will have the light of life."

Jesus is our dear friend for life! He is always walking alongside us in this life; we are never alone. He gives us this gift through the Holy Spirit to be a light. Because our burden is no longer heavy, we can walk joyfully! We are heirs of the light; it is our birthright to be rays of sunshine.

11

Lazarus

.

The song "Back to Life" by Bethel Music says, "I won't forget the moment I heard you call my name. Out of the grip of darkness into the light of grace. Just like Lazarus, oh, you brought me back to life."

Lazarus was a man of faith (I'm referring to John 11). And Jesus claimed that even though Lazarus died, he would live because He believed in Jesus. Jesus said, "I am the resurrection and the life. Even if he dies, the one who believes in me will live. Everyone who lives and believes in me will never die. Do you believe this?"

Lazarus was brought back to life! What a fantastic story. Imagine the gratitude that Lazarus felt for Jesus.

In my personal experience, I had gone so deep into darkness that I almost lost my life. I had just a glimmer of hope, and God pulled me out. He brought me back to life, back to my joyful self. Faith, even as small as a mustard seed, can move mountains. God's light of grace is whole! It has power over any grip of darkness we may have. Jesus says that we are his!

I will not forget the day God called me out of the darkness and into His light again. At the same time, I sincerely hope you will never feel that low and lost and will have just a glimmer of faith to pull you out! His grace abounds.

12

Resurrection Power

Did you know you have the power of the resurrection living in you right now? After the resurrection of Jesus, he gave us the gift of the Holy Spirit to live in our hearts. The Holy Spirit's power is life-altering. Romans 8:11 says, "And if the Spirit of him who raised Jesus from the dead lives in you, then he who raised Christ from the dead will also bring your mortal bodies to life through his Spirit who lives in you."

Take a moment to let that verse soak into your heart. His Spirit lives in us! There is a life worth living when you turn to the living Spirit of God; we experience a renewed hope. He will carry you out of your wilderness and darkness and bring you into His light! He has so much tender love in his heart for you!

God is our Father in Heaven who watches over our every step. When we trip and fall, He will help lift us back up. Consider it a joy to have gone through trials… For you have living hope in you! Living hope from the Holy Spirit lives inside of you! We can have hope for tomorrow and the mysteries of the future.

We were once dead in sin and despair, but there is LIFE in Him! Walk in fullness, knowing that God, who created this Earth, created and needed you in it!

13

Peachy

I have had two distinct moments when I have asked God about my purpose in life. The first time He told me that it was written in my name, who I am supposed to be: a "Ray" of light. The second time I was given this image of peaches in my mind, He delights in me. My purpose is to delight in the Lord and to focus on Him and His plan for me. When I turn to the Father and walk with Him, fruit will be produced and His light will shine.

Galatians 5:22-25 says, "But the fruit of the Spirit is love, joy, peace, patience, kindness, goodness, faithfulness, gentleness, and self-control. The law is not against such things. Now those who belong to Christ Jesus have crucified the flesh with its passions and desires. If we live by the Spirit, let us also keep in step with the Spirit."

I only want what God has in store for my life, because it is not fruitful when I try to make it my own.

When I actively walk with the Spirit, love exists, gentleness is there, and self-control is in practice. I am not saying it is always easy but worth it. I do not always need to question because I have confidence in what the Lord has in store.

God made you on purpose! You were beautifully made; the Lord delights in you! You are so important to Him. He formed you in your mother's womb with intention. You are magnificent in the eyes of God. I pray that you would embrace the purpose God has for your life.

14

There's a Little Light, Thank You, Jesus!

Psalm 119:105 says, "Your word is a lamp for my feet and a light on my path." We can rejoice in each step we take because it is in God's path. When we seek advice from Him on whether or not we should walk through the open door or close the door, it makes the decision so much easier!

Whatever your path may include, may it be only to bring glory to God. May you have fullness of joy, fun, and freedom. Our friend, Jesus, is walking alongside us! When light is shown on our path, we can thank Him! The light shines so bright that even in darkness, we will be able to see it, even if it is just a glimpse.

15

Lay Your Life Down

Did you know that nothing can separate us from God's love? Christ-like love is a command for us! Jesus said, "Love one another as I have loved you. No one has greater love than this: to lay down his life for his friends," John 15:12-13. He has loved us so greatly that He died for us. Nothing can separate us from that.

Before we can love one another, we must embrace and know how loved we are individually. Did you know that you are loved deeply? God is for you! You are His masterpiece. He loves you no matter what!

Now think of how life-changing His love is- do you love each person you meet with that same tenderness and compassion? How about the ones you are closest to? Do you remember that last time you said, "I love you," to the ones you love most? Love is kind and forgiving.

By remaining in Christ, we will experience the fullness of his love. To demonstrate that to other people is to demonstrate kindness, appreciation, and fondness. The best example of this love is Christ. He loves us all so much! He loves you so much!

Our lives are a reflection of God's grace and love for us. The love He has in store for you and the person next to you is never-ending.

16

Go Out Into the World

Jesus gives this commandment in Mark 16:15, "Go into all the world and preach the gospel to all creation." I used to think I needed a title before my name, such as "Ministry Director" or "Pastor," to do this. Jesus has called us all into ministry. Each of us has different ministries: our families, coworkers, classmates, or peers. Anyone you walk alongside in life is someone who deserves to hear about the love of Christ and experience it!

When I used to think I needed a specific title, I wasn't living in a way that honored God. My job position, volunteer position, or membership status does not define who I am. God has called me a "Daughter of a King," the only title I will ever carry.

I pray that God will soften our hearts towards the people He placed in our lives for a reason. May we show them what Christ-like love looks like and share with them the powerful Word of God. If you feel called to share the Good News with someone, do it! Do it with boldness, kindness, and love. Remember Joshua 1:9? Be courageous!

17

A Joyful Sound

Take a moment to read Psalm 100:

"Let the whole earth shout triumphantly to the Lord!
Serve the Lord with gladness;
come before him with joyful songs. Acknowledge
that the Lord is God.
He made us, and we are his—
his people, the sheep of his pasture. Enter his gates
with thanksgiving and his courts with praise. Give
thanks to him and bless his name. For the Lord is
good, and his faithful love endures forever; his
faithfulness, through all generations."

There is a lot to unpack with this Psalm. We
have so much to be joyous about and to celebrate!
We were made to worship the Lord! Worship Him
with joy on your face. Let His Spirit rest upon you
and bring you joy. There is joy in the trust we have in
Him! Having a thankful heart will allow us all to focus
on His goodness. I love being the Lord's sheep. Even

just thinking about how faithful His love is makes me want to bow in worship! I pray the same for you! Bring out those tambourines and flutes!

18

It's the Little Things

Colossians 3:16-17 says, "Let the word of Christ dwell richly among you, in all wisdom teaching and admonishing one another through psalms, hymns, and spiritual songs, singing to God with gratitude in your hearts. And whatever you do, in word or in deed, do everything in the name of the Lord Jesus, giving thanks to God the Father through him." This verse is one of my favorites and a great reminder of the life I want to live. A heart filled with gratitude is what I desire! Letting Christ's teaching dwell in your Spirit and living a life of worship will ultimately lead to joy!

It is a joy and a privilege to do everything in the name of the Lord Jesus. There is no one like Him, and He is so worthy of my life!

There was a time in my life when I started a gratitude journal. It started with vague thanksgiving, but then it became specific and precise in what I thanked God for. I was grateful for the air I breathed, for customers at work, and for the little things. What does gratitude look like to you? Are you singing with gratitude while doing your homework or taking out the trash? Even in the little things, there is something to be grateful for. A grateful heart is a joyful heart!

19

Ray of Light

Psalm 16:9-11 says, "Therefore my heart is glad and my whole being rejoices; my body also rests securely. For you will not abandon me to Sheol; you will not allow your faithful one to see decay. You reveal the path of life to me;
in your presence is abundant joy;
at your right hand are eternal pleasures". There is ease and joy in the presence of the Lord. There is freedom knowing that He will never abandon us. We do not need to live a life full of fear, anxiety, or shame. We are free because of the goodness of God and the blood shed on the cross!

When you rest in His goodness, His light will shine through you. The light from Christ will outshine any darkness or battle you could experience. Therefore, rejoice and be glad, because the Lord loves you so! The light in you is called to such greater things. The light shining through you will change the world. Be encouraged to know that!

When you fully trust Him, everything will fall into place. Peace and joy will come when it does not make sense to have.

Know this: God is all-present and a-knowing. In what may seem to be the darkest places, there will still be His light. It says in Psalm 139:12, "even the darkness is not dark to you. The night shines like the day; darkness and light are alike to you". You do not need to fret when you walk in the fullness of God and His plan for your life. Nothing is too dark for the Lord to walk you out of and into the light. The Creator of the Heavens and the Earth loves you so much that He sent His son as the ultimate example of being a light. There is joy in walking with the Father!

20

My Cup Overflows

One of my favorite Psalms, Psalm 23, displays the image of fully trusting in the goodness of God and knowing that He is enough!

"The Lord is my shepherd;
I have what I need. He lets me lie down in green pastures; he leads me beside quiet waters. He renews my life; he leads me along the right paths for his name's sake. Even when I go through the darkest valley, I fear no danger,
for you are with me; your rod and your staff—they comfort me. You prepare a table before me in the presence of my enemies; you anoint my head with oil; my cup overflows. Only goodness and faithful love will pursue me
all the days of my life, and I will dwell in the house of the Lord as long as I live."

The line in that passage, "My cup overflows," jumps out to me in this moment. When I imagine

God pouring into my cup, I see peace, joy, kindness, compassion, and love pouring into it. He pours until the cup is overflowing. Before I know it, I am covered in peace, joy, kindness, compassion, and love to the point that I can only ever show that to others!

He pours His goodness and faithfulness into our hearts again and again. He never leaves our side! The goodness of God will never fail us. We have all we need when we trust Jesus; He will provide for us! The beauty of His love is that it will always remain and abound.

When we fully comprehend that God loves us, we will walk joyfully. It will have us skipping down the path! We have the honor of dwelling in the fullness of His Spirit. What a joy that is! Nothing (and I mean, NOTHING) will ever make you undeserving of God's love. Nothing will stop the goodness of God from running after you! His heart is for you. I pray that you would be anointed with His Spirit and experience the joy that Christ has given us!

21

A Ribbon of Grace

Colossians 3:12-15 says. "Therefore, as God's chosen ones, holy and dearly loved, put on compassion, kindness, humility, gentleness, and patience, bearing with one another and forgiving one another if anyone has a grievance against another. Just as the Lord has forgiven you, you are also to forgive. Above all, put on love, the perfect bond of unity. And let the peace of Christ, to which you were also called in one body, rule your hearts. And be thankful."

We are commanded to live with peace, love, and forgiveness ruling our hearts. That may not always be easy, but it becomes easier when we understand the grace God has blessed us with. When we hold on to hurt and anger towards someone, we carry a burden that we should not. Whatever or whoever you may struggle with forgiving should be treated with the knowledge that Jesus also died for them. We can also rely on the strength of God to help us forgive when it is hard.

To put love on your sleeve is to love all who come into your path. Grace should be extended to all. Grace, love, hope, and peace should be overflowing from our hearts. Let those rule your heart!

22

Children of God

1 John 3 starts with, "See what great love the Father has given us that we should be called God's children —and we are!" All of us are His children! What a beautiful gift that is!

To be a child is to be full of wonder and awe! God loves it when we have child-like faith. Trust in God; He will provide and make a way for us. Child-like faith is gentle, fun, and pure. Take a moment to let His fatherly love for you sink in. Cherish it!

I John 3 also reminds me that the people I cross paths with are God's children. Whoever I see in a day is fully known and loved! They are my brother or sister in Christ, and I am to love them.

23

In All You Do

Colossians 3:23-24, "Whatever you do, work at it with all your heart, as working for the Lord, not for human masters, since you know that you will receive an inheritance from the Lord as a reward. It is the Lord Christ you are serving."

In serving the Lord, we are to do it with a gracious heart. In all we do, we are supposed to do it with all of our heart, praising God while we do it. While doing the laundry, working, studying, and so on.

All that we do includes all our interactions with other people. Are we meeting the people we interact with daily with love? Are we serving them with a grateful heart?

24

Unconditional

God's love for you knows no bounds. There is no performance or expectation from us, but to accept His love. Luke 15 shares the parable of the lost sheep. The same love and joyfulness that comes to a shepherd finding his lost sheep is the same when we run to the Father. The shepherd said, "Rejoice with me, because I have found my lost sheep!" God is happy when we turn to him. His love is after us!

God's love for us is patient, kind, and forgiving. 1 John 4:18-19 says, "There is no fear in love; instead, perfect love drives out fear, because fear involves punishment. So the one who fears is not complete in love. We love because he first loved us." Fear cannot exist in our hearts when we let the love of God consume us! God's love reveals that we can trust Him, experience complete peace, and be confident in who He made us to be. God loves you, and so much is in store for you.

www.ingramcontent.com/pod-product-compliance
Lightning Source LLC
Chambersburg PA
CBHW061720120626
46550CB00003B/1301